The Gospel And AUTISM:

Living as God intended with a unique wiring

By. Zachary Chapman

PUBLISHERS NOTE: This is a work of Non-Fictional background. Several quotes from real world people and the Bible are used in this book.

Lulu Press, Inc
627 Davis Dr
Suite 300
Morrisville, NC
www.lulu.com

Published under accordance with Zachary Chapman. First published in USA by Zachary Chapman in 2020

Printed in the USA

Dedicated to all those who suffer from autism and look to Jesus as their savior.

Table of Contents

CHAPTER 1

What are disabilities?

The Bible doesn't address what disabilities are directly. However, it does explain how we are to treat those with disabilities in general. It says in John 9:1-3 "As he passed by, he saw a man blind from birth. And his disciples asked him, "Rabbi, who sinned, this man or his parents, that he was born blind?" Jesus answered, "It was not that this man sinned, or his parents, but that the works of God might be displayed in him."

We all seem to have this switch that turns on and makes us think that disabilities come from sinning. Therefore, we tend to say, "You really messed up." Or "Your parents must've had some problems." And that's just not cool.

Yes, we have freewill, but that doesn't mean we are the cause of our disabilities. Genes can sometimes just form funny. That's not our fault.

We need to start teaching the younger generation what disability really means. The definition is, "Any condition that makes it more difficult for a person to do certain things and activities or interact with the world around them." Nowhere in the definition does it say that we are the cause of disabilities. Disabilities are just a part of getting to be on Earth.

Disabilities are part of our imperfection, but they aren't the cause. We tend to blame disabilities for our imperfection. Imperfection and disabilities may have a part to play with one another, but they are not connected.

We purposely choose to sin. That alone is why we are imperfect. Humans choose to rape, steal, and murder. Disabilities don't do that. We willingly disobey the ten commandments.

That being said, what disabilities can do is cause us to not see things through all the way. They can be very disorienting and misleading. Like for instance, my friend Luke has auditory processing disorder (APD). Which is a disorder that makes it hard to interpret sounds and words. It's caused by a dysfunction in the central nervous system. He sometimes takes things differently than what they actually are. It sucks because it's not his fault. And we would often have arguments over him not understanding fully.

We would constantly make fun of each other's disorder, any way we could. It was very sad because we were both well into our teens and we were acting like five-year-old's. This is unfortunately what happens when you don't try to control your disorder.

I have another friend named Marshall who suffers from Tourette Syndrome which makes it difficult for him to be still for long periods of time. He and I used to fight a lot in-part because we didn't have our disabilities sorted out. How could we? We were just young lads. The truth is we really could have been better if we had realized how old we really were. We met when I was ten, Marshall was seven. At first being that young and fighting is understandable. However, we fought for YEARS. It wasn't until about two years ago we actually grew older and stopped our pointless fights.

Some of the pointless fights would unfortunately come from our disorders. For example, like I said earlier, Tourette syndrome causes Marshall to move a lot. And sometimes he would accidently touch me in a way that felt like an attack. Other times my autism would kick in and I would start getting upset over small things like, Marshall looking over at my tablet to see what game I was playing. Pretty stupid right?

Well if you are autistic, this can be very unnerving, so watch out for that. I'd say it's okay to call someone out, but whatever you do, don't turn it into very strong discipline.

Okay, enough rambling on about the negative effects of disabilities. Let's look at the positives. A good example is the disorder that's the main topic of this book. Autism may make some people hyperactive, or not completely understand the world around them. However, it also may mean that you are likely much smarter than the average person. I mean, look at Bill Gates and what he's done. It is thought that he has something on the autism spectrum, I believe it's Asperger's Syndrome, which is what I have. And that is partly how he's been able to do the things he's done.

Autistic people in some circumstances can be VERY fast learners. Not just by watching and listening to lectures or real-life situations, but also by figuring things out by themselves. That's pretty dope. Whenever you're able to teach yourself something without any help, that's remarkable. And that's exactly what loads of autistic people are notorious for.

Being an autistic man myself. I have many of the positive traits of the disorder. Not to brag but, I indeed have some super smarts. I really hate my disability sometimes. Other times though, I thank God himself for bestowing such gifts to me.

Our disabilities are not burdens. On the contrary, they are gifts. They are what make us more unique than everyone else. Though they may trouble us at times, they are not meant to be taken lightly. Once we know how to use them to our advantage, we can become revolutionary.

It says in the Bible that we are not to take Gods gifts as a burden, but to cherish them and use them to their fullest ability. It's written in 2 Timothy 1:6-7 "For this reason I remind you to fan into flame the gift of God, which is in you through the laying on of my hands, for God gave us a spirit not of fear but of power and love and self-control."

In the following chapter, we will be talking about autism itself. What is it? What does it do? How do we deal with it?

CHAPTER 2

What is Autism?

Let's talk about autism. What is it? The definition is: Autism is a disorder characterized by difficulties with social interaction and communication, and by restricted and repetitive behavior.

What does autism do? Like it says in the definition, autism affects behavior, and communication. For example, lots of people with autism tend to be on a strict schedule and if that schedule is changed just slightly, even if it's once, this can take someone with autism over the edge.

Another good example is something I've experienced in the past. Which is not knowing when to stop talking. I recently saw a video on YouTube by SBSK that explains this in perfect detail. The main guy, Chris, interviewed a very sweet young autistic girl named Ellie who has a lot of the same traits I do.

I was obsessed with kid shows until I was about fourteen years old. And I would constantly want to talk about them at the dinner table or with friends whenever we'd go out to eat. So, what had to start happening is someone (in my case, my dad), would step in and change the subject. At first, I didn't take it too well. To my non-surprise, neither did Ellie, but as it keeps happening and the more you got used to it, it becomes more bearable and you understand why It's happening. Don't feel bad when your kid or whoever it may be doesn't appreciate the help at first. It's going to take some time for them to get used to it and understand that you're not doing it to cut them off. Just make sure when you do change the subject, make sure it's something else relevant to their life. I remember from the SBSK video, Ellie's mom explained how she would say something like "Oh, what about that picture you drew?" something among those lines.

Those are just a few examples of how autism affects people and how to handle those situations. I hope so far, you've seen what disability really is, and what autism really is. Before I wrap up this chapter, I'd like to take a moment to read some more scripture about how we should treat people who are extremely unique.

First one I want to cover is Joshua 1:9 "Have I not commanded you? Be strong and courageous. Do not be frightened and do not be dismayed, for the Lord your God is with you wherever you go." I wanted to cover this verse because of the significance it holds. Whenever situations happen that seem like it's going to end the world, we almost instinctively blame God for it. Like the recent outbreak of the coronavirus. I've heard that loads of people are either blaming God for creating the virus, or just sitting back on his behind and letting the virus take its course. We don't take into account that God gave us freewill. With that freewill we commit sin. That's what creates these deadly viruses, not God.

Now I know a lot of people are going to get on me for what I said earlier in the book. About how we as sinners aren't the cause of disorders. In my mind, there is a big difference between disorder and disease. A disease isn't exactly something your born with. It's something you catch from out in the open. Like the coronavirus or an STD or even the common cold.

There are diseases we can catch from our mothers during pregnancy. Like deformities for example. Now I know there will be a lot of controversy about this topic because someone could easily say "Well, some people are born with tumors growing all over their bodies. Isn't that a deformity? You have no place to talk."

Let me tell you something, if tumors were a deformity, every single one would make us look weird. There are loads of people that have brain tumors that don't show through. We only know they're there because of technology. So no, in my mind, tumors are not a deformity. They may affect the way we look based on how they grow, but they do not come from something that happened during our mother's pregnancy.

There is something called an NF gene. And no, that has nothing to do with the greatest rapper on the planet. An NF gene is a gene that feeds protein to the body to keep tumors from being produced. Like I said early on, sometimes gene's just form funny. And when that happens to an NF gene, the gene isn't able to produce the protein needed to keep the body from producing tumors. This is another great story I saw from SBSK. Chris interviewed a guy named Reggie who suffers from a disorder called neurofibromatosis. Which is literally what I just got done describing. Be sure to check that one out on YouTube, and comment on the video what your favorite type of cake is. Reggie is a baker. If you need a cake or pie, he's got you covered.

The next verse I want to cover is Leviticus 19:14 "You shall not curse a deaf man, nor place a stumbling block before the blind, but you shall revere the Lord your God. I am the Lord." We hear all the time these crazy people bashing the disabled. It goes from being bullied in school, to getting robbed and never noticing. It's sad to see people this way and it needs to change.

We need more people to stand up for the disabled and preach this verse to those who bash them. We can fix this mess. It's just going to take work.

"Ugh, work, why?" I know, I know, work isn't a human strong suit. It is, however, very effective. If the work you do for a business gets you a good amount of green paper, you'd be surprised by what could happen by working for God. MIRACLES CAN HAPPEN. You just got to believe and have faith.

In the next few chapters I'm going to tell my life story of how I got diagnosed, what I went through to conquer it. And how it affected others around me. Sit back, grab your popcorn, and get comfy. It's a very big story.

CHAPTER 3

My Experience (My life story) Part: 1

So, I have had autism traits starting at birth. As an infant I would regularly get upset at small things like, running out of formula, or not having enough time with my binky.

Of course, at that time, my parents just thought that was normal baby behavior. I'm an only child. So obviously I was my parent's first kid. So, they had no prior experience to what baby behavior was like except for hanging around my cousins. Who are two years older than I am.

Long story short, when my aunt was about to give birth to my twin cousins, she had some difficulties. So, my mom, bless her heart, drove all the way up from Orlando to Atlanta in an instant to help my auntie out. My mom was one of the first people to ever hold my cousins after they were born. Okay, back to me.

So that's how my parents got their very little experience with infants. As I got to be about a year old some of the traits became more apparent. My parents still didn't think much of it because they thought it was normal. It wasn't until I got into pre-school at age four, that someone actually had suspicions.

One day while playing on the playground, my teacher noticed

something different about me. That afternoon she brought it up to my parents and needless to say, they were pretty weirded out that someone would say something like that about their child.

In the moment they didn't think a lot more than just "Why would someone say something like that about our son?" It took a few weeks, but eventually they noticed that the behavior my teacher described was actually there. So, they took me to a pediatrics office where I was officially diagnosed with Asperger's syndrome. Which is a disability that used to be listed on the autism spectrum.

Nowadays Asperger's is in a category all by itself. I still consider it a form of autism because of all the similar traits. Like repeating things over and over, or hyperactive movements such as hand shaking and jumping. I began experiencing more and more traits of my disorder while ending out pre-school and starting elementary school.

I started kindergarten when I was five. I had a great deal of fun until about halfway through the first month in. It all changed when out of nowhere in the middle of class a VERY LOUD horn sound started racing through the classroom. I was experiencing my very first fire drill. Oh my, even writing those words makes me quiver. I remember being completely traumatized by the whole thing. It was then that I first discovered I had a fear of loud noises. Later on in my life I would self-diagnose myself with phonophobia (the fear of loud sounds) which is very common among autistic kids.

When the drill ended, I remember needing to be rushed to the counselor's office crying my eyes out with everyone in my class and the classes neighboring laughing their heads off at me. That was my first ever experience with bullying.

I ended up having to have the school counselor come into my class multiple times a week to make sure

I was okay. It was also being done because after that day, I could never focus in class because I would be so worried about the fire alarm sounding. Even when I knew it wasn't drill day, I would still worry about it malfunctioning or there being a real emergency. It got so bad that I would constantly get teased about it and nothing was done to stop it.

Eventually my parents were told of the incident and they spoke to the school about an IEP plan. That really helped me in a few situations. Like on drill days, or days where we would have mechanics working on the system. I would be taken into a small quiet room with no fire alarm in it to do my work. So I wouldn't be so startled when the alarm sounded. But that still didn't help my fear of it going off at other times. The truth is, you never know when the fire alarm is going to sound. And this carried on with me not just at school. After that first incident, anywhere I would go that had fire alarms around would always make me cover my ears.

It made my life miserable. My grades declined very steadily moving forward. I was constantly bullied by my peers, and I could never stop going over the edge. Overall that schoolyear was so bad, I inevitably got held back. Which would be a weight that I still today carry on my shoulders.

That summer I was forced to go to summer school which didn't help me any. The only good thing that came out of it was the fact that we only had one fire alarm incident, and it happened while everyone was already outside. The work we had to do had no relevance to anything we'd learned during the schoolyear or anything we'd need moving forward.

The beginning of my second year of kindergarten wasn't much better. It was literally just a repeat of the previous year and even though it was hard to pay attention I still knew what everything was. The only reason they really held me back besides my autism was the fact that I didn't have the best handwriting. Which makes no sense to me because most five to six-year-olds don't have the best handwriting.

The bullying didn't ease up either. There was this one particular kid who made me his punching bag from kindergarten, all the way to fifth grade. He knew all my flaws, fears, and everything negative about me. He took all that to his advantage and bullied me horrifically. Especially when fire drills would happen, but it didn't stop there.

This kid would physically and verbally abuse me. He would make fun of me and my family anyway he could. I remember distinctly him once saying "Your mom is mean, your dad is ugly, and your grandparents are old creeps, just like you." He was not a friendly camper. And because of my autism, I would always fight back with remarks that would get me into trouble.

I would throw punches (luckily, I always missed), talk back to people, and disobey direct orders from teachers. It was almost impossible for me to ignore anything thrown at me. And that's literally all I was told to do when someone did something to me. No one understood that for someone in my condition that ignoring and brushing it off was just not a capability.

It was also early that schoolyear when my mom came home one

night and told me she was leaving. This wasn't at all helpful. It made me even more unable to focus in class and at home.

Fast forward to second grade. My grades were still steadily declining, I had been still unable to pay close attention because of my phonophobia, and the bullying never stopped. It was a nightmare.

I almost never could complete full piles of schoolwork, and homework I was forced against my will to complete, I'd get a splitting headache every day, and my family would always be mad at me because they didn't understand. I was often put in a time out chair or sent to a corner for not doing homework. And the simple truth is, I COULDN'T. I didn't have the capacity with everything going on. My parents had been divorced, my phonophobia was at an all-time high, my peers all picked on me, my teachers didn't care at all, and my family and I were not getting along in the slightest.

Later on in the schoolyear, I'm having a really bad day. With everything that had happened over the last few years, I had become severely depressed. I was coming home from school in tears each day. I would try to fake being happy so my family wouldn't worry. Nothing good was happening in my life.

That day, I was out at recess minding my own business, when that one kid started chasing me around the playground. He eventually caught up with me and shoved me into a tree, almost cutting up my face. My autism kicked in with my fight or flight response and I punched him in the chest. He then proceeded to run toward the teachers.

At that moment I was just done. I was done with everything, my peers all hated me, I was constantly afraid, my teachers didn't care about my autism, or anything for that matter, my family and I could not see eye to eye, and I was the one always paying for everything. I just couldn't take it anymore, I was hopeless, depressed, and alone. So, without any hesitation, it was that moment, I attempted to take my life.

CHAPTER 4

My Experience (My life story) Part: 2

Though I was unhappy about it, I was very lucky to have failed. My teacher came up from behind me and grabbed me. She asked me what I was doing, and I told her the truth. She immediately took me to the front office where I waited for hours to first have a talk with the nurse, then my counselor, then the vice principal. It was awful.

All I was told was how stupid I was for punching another kid and then trying to get out of it. They thought my suicide attempt was just a way to distract the teachers from what I'd just done and a way to escape the punishment. I kept on wishing I'd have gone through with it quicker. I wouldn't have been in that situation if I had. No one understood. And I couldn't explain it to anyone because A: I didn't know how. And B: No one would ever listen.

When my parents finally got called, they were the first ones to actually ask if I was okay. I told them no. The vice-principle told them not to baby me because I wasn't innocent. That really ticked me off. My parents didn't believe them thankfully and they took me home.

That night I told them everything I could about how I felt. They all hugged me and apologized for everything they had done and promised to get me help. Well, soon enough, they did.

A few months later they took me to a counseling office in Winter Park, Florida to have me sit down one on one with a personal counselor and have them assess me. My counselor's name was Mrs. Christine. I will always have a special place in my heart for her. She was the first person who really understood me. She has a son of her own who has Asperger's. So, she knew exactly how I felt and just how to treat me. She spoke to my family and things were finally set in motion to better my life.

I still had to go to that wretched elementary school until I graduated. I still had my complications, but thanks to Mrs. Christine, I had ways to cope with them. And with much difficulty, I was able to finish elementary school. That summer I truly rejoiced. No more torture from those hooligans, no more insults from teachers, and no more restless nights of trying to get homework done. I was at peace for the first time in a very long time. It was at this time I really started to see positive change in my life.

God was showing me that I had been through enough crap for a while and he wanted to reward me. He gave me help. I learned this verse around this time, Isaiah 41:10 "So do not fear, for I am with you; do not be dismayed, for I am your God. I will strengthen you and help you; I will uphold you with my righteous right hand." It was a reminder that no matter what I was going through, God was with me and he had my back.

Over the course of that summer my dad had found a special needs school right by my house. And that, was the biggest blessing I'd received in my life at the time.

CHAPTER 5

My Experience (My life story) Part: 3

My first day of middle school arrived. It was a bit unnerving because it was a new place, new people, and a new environment. It took quite a few days to actually get used to the changes, but once I did, I was in heaven compared to what I faced just one schoolyear prior. No one bullied me, I was welcomed with open arms, and the work was INCREDIBLY easy.

It was super easy to make friends. I had people I could relate to, and I had a much better administration to look up to. My counselor was actually caring and loved all us unique kids.

I was top of my class for as long as I was there. I was an ace at P.E. and math the most. I hear that the majority of autistic kids are really good at math. I guess I inherited that trait. I mean, straight A's in all math subjects up until the eleventh grade.

The best part was, for my first year of junior high they had a policy where if you had issues with loud sounds you were taken out of certain activities, INCLUDING fire drills. So, for my sixth-grade year, everything was perfect.

I distinctly remember my friend Julian, he and I were both big fans of the Ninja Turtles, and pizza. We'd spend every snack and lunch break discussing the Ninja Turtles nickelodeon series and the movie that had come out that year. We also bonded over Minecraft.

Which by the way, If your autistic, I highly recommend you give Minecraft a try. It's a great way to challenge yourself and get your mind working in ways you never thought possible. I mean the aim of the regular game mode is to survive and build. You have to know what it takes to build what, and how to keep yourself safe from danger. Both of those are great examples of things we experience in everyday life. It also involves a lot of skill from real life. Like science for example, you need to have ingredients to cook certain foods. You need to mix certain chemicals to create certain compounds. It's a great way for an autistic mind which already has great potential to gain even more knowledge and skillsets.

My sixth-grade year went so smoothly it was unbelievable. I'd finally seen what God could do with someone who had experienced literal hell in their past. That Easter, I'd gotten to witness an amazing performance and message at the sunrise service at SeaWorld. And it was there that I said "Jesus, I want to accept you as my lord and savior."

After the service, I told my dad what I wanted to do. So, the next day our church had their Easter service. And that night, our pastor prayed the prayer of salvation with me. And I couldn't have been happier. I knew where I was going to spend eternity after I die. I would get to be in the presence of God himself. That really put me at ease.

Over the summer I did more and more stuff to get stronger in my faith. I found the type of Christian music that resonated with me. I found my favorite Christian YouTubers, and I made the biggest decision that in my mind was bigger than just accepting Christ. I decided, to get baptized.

As the summer came to an end, I was thrilled with everything that had happened. I was a firm believer, I was in a great school, my family and I were finally close again, things could not get any better. That soon changed when school restarted that fall.

In seventh grade a couple things happened that didn't really help my situation. Julian moved to another school, and they took away the student loud noise policy because we got a new principle. So, I unfortunately lost a good friend, and I just had to suck it up whenever it was fire drill day. Which really brought back some old fears from elementary school.

If you ask me, they shouldn't do fire drills once you get to middle school. Because after doing fire drills for five straight years, I'd say the students know what to do when they hear that alarm sound.

I still was seeing Mrs. Christine and the coping mechanisms she gave me worked fine for a good amount of time. I was able to stick it out when fire drills happened from that point on. I also got some advice from her that really helped my education. I got my homework done on time, all the time, no matter what the situation.

Moving onto the eighth grade, that was probably my best year academically in junior high. The one thing I could not stand my eighth-grade year was my math teacher. It had nothing to do with the work. I aced all the work. It was her in general.

She would seem very light and bubbly when you first walked in the room, but once class began, she turned into someone who didn't know how to treat special needs kids. She treated us like we were all regular public-school kids.

She never once took into account that we all learned differently. Kids were always getting in trouble in her class, not because they were misbehaving, but because she didn't know how to teach their certain disorder. She'd also a lot of times expect us to figure out work on our own instead of teaching us. And while some people (me included) got the work without a lecture, others just couldn't crack it. And that really got some people on the teacher's bad side.

She would constantly be taking kids out into the hall to have a "serious talk" with them about their academic performance. That really ticked me off. I did everything I could to never interact with that teacher. Sometimes I had no choice cause she'd either call me up to do a problem, or other times I'd be the first one in the classroom and she'd have no one else to talk to, but ninety-nine percent of the time, I was purely quiet.

There was one day where I had just had enough of fighting in that class. So, I got up and shouted, "SHUT THE FRICK UP." And that was a huge mistake. You see, this teacher never heard what really came out of kids mouths half the time. So, when I said that, she immediately stormed over to my desk and said "Get in the hall right now. Were going to talk."

She just assumed that I dropped the F bomb without asking anyone else what they had heard or took time to process what she'd just heard. So she took me out into the hall and we had a very distinctive conversation about how I had screwed up and she apparently heard everything quote on quote, "PERFECTLY." I tried to tell her the truth, but she was just not having it. Luckily, I got off the hook with just a warning, but the effect it had on me was so severe, I actually took the hit. And later that day I went to the Dean's office and told him a flat out lie, just to try and make my teacher happy. See, I'm a perfectionist. I don't like upsetting people. So instead of doing what I should've done, which was tell the Dean what really happened. I instead lied about myself just to try and make someone else happy.

There's a very valuable lesson I learned from this experience. And that is, you can't make others happy, you can only make yourself happy. I wish I'd known that before I did what I did. I would've immediately gone to the Dean's office and testified against that teacher. Not lied about the situation to make her happy. I wasn't even her biggest fan to begin with.

Okay, moving on. Besides that one experience my final year of junior high went extremely well. I made some new friends, and had a great relationship with the school in general.

Graduation day came and I felt so accomplished. Only four more years had to go by before I was free. I got to stand by all my friends as we rejoiced getting our diploma's. I couldn't think of a better way to end out the year.

That summer though, wasn't very relaxing and fun. Because I was entering high school, they had a ton of assignments that we had to complete before going back in the fall. I of course did all the work, but I nearly killed myself doing it.

I was staying up night after night till three in the morning working on those assignments. There was that much. I'd pay for all that work mentally in the coming months. Let's just say, I was in no way prepared for what I was about to face.

CHAPTER 6

My Experience (My life story) Part: 4

Now it was time for the biggest academic challenge I would face yet, Every kids' worst nightmare, "HIGH SCHOOL." Oh boy, where to begin. I guess I'll start with what I'd faced the first day.

The first day went pretty smooth until lunch time. My first block, I had tried to welcome a new student. And at lunch time, I introduced him to a group of people I thought he would fit in really well with. And he did. But little did I know what I just did would come back to bite me in the behind.

This new kid was cocky as could be. He would never shut up about how many girls he'd been in bed with and how excellent he was at baseball. And whenever he would find someone that hadn't had that kind of quote on quote "success" he'd make them his little chew toys.

And unfortunately, that turned out to be me, and my best friend.

We were constant victims of his teasing and insults. And sadly, I still hadn't gotten full control of my autism. So, I would constantly fight back with things I'd never say. Words were coming out of my mouth that I'd never said before. It was not good.

On top of that, I once again had the teacher I'd had the previous year for math, this year for science. And she was so much worse than the year before. We had to do a science project for the school science fair, and she basically shot down every idea we had. It was what she wanted, or we flunked. So that was not at all helpful to anyone.

As the year went on. This kid who had been bullying me and my best friend had gotten together a huge group of minions who obeyed his every word. I started thinking, "This kid clearly has some issues. Why on Earth would they let him in this school without proof of a learning disability?" I had found out from a third-party source that the school had let him in without a proof of diagnoses. And when I found out why I was so shocked.

It was our principle. I again learned from a third-party source that our principle had planned to take the school down a mainstream path. Which would mix both special needs kids, with regular kids.

You can probably see all the issues with that. People send their learning disability kids to a special needs school to get them away from regular kids who bully and torture them. And somehow our principle thinks the best way to end bullying is to bring the kids together because she thinks that it will teach the regular kids respect. Once I had this information, I immediately started coming up with a plan to get out of that school.

By the end of that schoolyear, I had had enough of all that schools' crap. I was getting back to the state I was in back in elementary school. I was experiencing depressive episodes and my grades were starting to plummet.

That summer they had given us another one of those huge assignments. And once again, I spent sleepless nights trying to get it all done. I almost didn't that summer. That's when I realized that they weren't just trying to make the student body mainstream, but the work as well.

When tenth grade started to my relief, that one kid and his pack were either gone, or with different people. Needless to say, I wasn't bothered by anyone anymore. I would sit alone at lunch, all the classes were intense because of the mainstream transition, and I was spiraling out of control. By that January I started to have suicidal thoughts again. Everything weighing on me was just too much.

The school didn't care that the work was beyond my capacity. I was the school introvert, so I didn't have but maybe one or two friends. And worst of all, I kept this all deep down inside me. I never talked about it with anyone which was not healthy. And by March, I'd reached my breaking point.

I finally spilled the beans to my dad about how I felt. And I told him that if I didn't get help, I would kill myself soon. So, my dad immediately got me an appointment setup the next day with Mrs. Christine. And she came to my rescue. She referred me to a different therapist named Mr. Nate and I started getting all my thoughts out with him.

There was only one problem. I'd never really talked about my past or present with anyone. So even though I was getting help. All the built-up memories had turned me into a complete wreck. There were multiple times I came close to attempting to end my life again. So, I said enough is enough, and I told my dad about what the principle had planned for the school.

Immediately we started looking for a homeschool program that would suit me. And we found one. So, as the schoolyear came to a close, my dad had the school transfer my transcripts, and that was that. I was finally once again free from hell.

Over that summer I finally had no assignments to complete and I could finally rest easy again. I praised God daily. For he had seen me through this darkness and pulled me back into the light. There was however a sequence of events coming up that would really mess me up.

Eleventh grade starts. And I'm super stoked about my new adventure. My buddy Marshall also started that same program. So, we spent the first day on facetime helping each other out on where to go and what to do. It was awesome.

We each only have one live class a day. Which made getting work done so much easier. And best of all, NO FIRE DRILLS.

Everything was great. That soon changed after the first month.

Even though this was a homeschool program. It was not special needs. So, I was getting three to four assignments a day and only having twelve hours to do each one. This didn't settle well with me. And before I knew it, I was falling behind.

This really got to me because I couldn't bear the thought of not being ahead. Ever since I got held back in kindergarten, I made it my mission to earn that year back. So, I fought with everything in me to get back on track, but I couldn't do it. And it turned into me getting more and more depressed, sleep deprived, stressed, and just overall not good. It was then that I knew I needed more help.

The next day I went to my dad and told him truthfully that my suicidal thoughts were worse than ever, and I needed more help. So, after talking to Mr. Nate, we went to a psychiatrist who referred me to a behavioral hospital. I honestly thought "Yes, this is where I can unplug from the world and get back on my feet." I hate to say it, but I was wrong.

My first day at that facility was catastrophically overwhelming and only made matters worse. They threw me into classes where I knew no one and gave me schoolwork that I had no idea how to do. And the teachers didn't help me one bit. I was so disoriented that I just sat and watched group therapy without participating. And I didn't even get one on one therapy. I literally just sat and tried not to sob all day. During recreation time. I just sat on the sofa in the rec room and held myself together the best I could.

As soon as the day was over and My dad picked me up, the second I got in the car I broke down worse than I had my entire life. I mean this place was full of people who didn't treat you like humans, the school system sucked. And Honestly, they should've never put me in the school environment because that is what got me to where I was in the first place. I mean, they never took into account that I had Asperger's. So, I was expected to know everything like a regular kid. The food was poorly made, and I didn't get to see my therapist. I tried to explain what had happened to my dad, but he tried everything he could to convince me that I should give it a few more days. I couldn't do that. So, after hours of begging and begging. He finally agreed that we would walk into the evaluation office in the morning and talk to someone. Which is exactly what we did.

We got to the facility the next day, and we happened to run into the guy who's in charge of the place. We asked to speak to him, and he brought us to the conference room. We sat down, and I told the whole story.

I explained how everything went down. And sadly, we found

out that everything I went through was actually intentional. They purposely put you in an unknown environment to rattle your cage. And you purposely didn't get to see your personal therapist on the first day or the next few days. My dad and I were appalled by this. We immediately told the guy we were pulling out. He wasn't very happy to hear that, but he didn't fight us. He got us the discharge papers, and we went on our merry way.

After that whole ordeal, we immediately got an appointment with Mr. Nate to discuss our next move. We got me back into my school program, and we came up with a happiness plan that I still am using today.

And since that plan has been set into motion I've been in a much better place. And my autism isn't keeping me down anymore either. I'm finally for the first time in my life, a REAL happy camper.

And that's my story. In the next chapter I'm going to discuss what I've learned from this journey and where I am now.

CHAPTER 7

What I've Learned!!

Growing up with this disorder as you can tell, was not very easy. I had a ton of up's and downs, but in the end, I'm still here. So, here is what I've learned from my experience.

Starting from what I went through as an infant. Now that I'm older, I'm much more mature when it comes to getting upset about things. I've learned that sometimes life throws you curveballs, and you need to choose to duck, or swing. Well, I've chosen to swing. For I know God will keep me safe. It says in scripture, Deuteronomy 33:12 "Of Benjamin he said, "May the beloved of the lord dwell in security by Him, Who shields him all the day, and he dwells between his shoulders.""

For people with autism, small things tend to seem big. What I've learned from experiencing this, is that there needs to be a change from both sides of the equation. The one suffering from autism must learn coping skills, and the person or thing causing the small problem that's upsetting them must cut them some slack. This means no more firing back when the autistic kid or adult gets upset at something unless you know they aren't practicing the coping skills.

On the topic of coping skills, I've learned that you must take the coping skills seriously, if you want any change in your dynamic. I'll go into more detail on coping skills in the next chapter, but for now, let me explain what happens if you don't take the coping skills seriously.

It is impossible to get better at controlling your autism without coping skills. What coping skills do is relax the body enough to where you can get a grip on yourself. I used to not take coping skills seriously because I didn't want to get a grip on myself. I thought the coping skills were just excuses to distract yourself from the situation. I especially did this when it came to fire drills. I never did any coping skills because I thought the teachers were just trying to distract me from what was about to happen. Once I actually tried the coping skills, I was surprised. I was actually relaxed, and when the fire alarm sounded it still startled me, but it didn't throw me over the cliff like it usually would. Here is what the Bible says about coping skills, Philippians 4:12-13

"Be aware, be warned, and be exhorted that, if we have any desire to overcome faults, if we sincerely desire to be in God's Kingdom, if we desire to be like God and glorify Him, we need to protect our relationship with him."

That's a great piece of advice. Something else I'll go over in the next chapter.

Something else I've learned from my experience is that It's sometimes very easy to forget things when your autistic. I've had a few instances while writing this book where I completely forgot about my everyday life. Like school, and work. The night I wrote this chapter I completely forgot that a co-worker was on vacation and I forgot to cover their shift. I had quite a few people upset with me. So, as much fun as it was writing this book. I've learned to never let ANYTHING get in the way of your real life.

I want to address that this was no one's fault, but mine. I'm the one who took it upon myself to completely shove my job out of my mind. Unfortunately, I've learned that even though autistic people tend to forget things when they're preoccupied, that's no excuse to not go about your daily life.

I've learned that being autistic is not a burden. God made me the way I am for a reason, and I'm grateful. I've learned how to use autism to my advantage when it comes to my real life. I'm able to figure out problems, address them, and solve them. It's really cool how as you grow and your brain develops, you can figure out things on your own that you thought were absurd. I've personally seen myself solve all sorts of problems, from schoolwork, to technology, and modern real-world issues.

I think that's enough rambling about nonsense. I just wanted to share my take on my experience as an autistic person. In the final chapter, I will be discussing what you can do whether you suffer from autism or not, to better help yourself or a loved one who struggles with autism.

CHAPTER 8

What Can You Do?

Let's start with how you should figure out if your child, friend, or loved one has autism. As a parent, autism should be very easy to spot if you know what you are looking for. Look for these signs if you have an infant. Struggles with daily activities, Sensitivity to change or small situations, Repetitive behaviors, trouble with communication, attachment to things, and struggles to grow and develop mentally.

These are all things I struggled with as an infant, up to about age four. That's when I started pre-school. Some things carried on until later in my life.

Here is what you should do at that stage. If you believe your child has autism, immediately take them to their pediatrician and have them refer you to a specialist who does autism tests and diagnoses. If your child has autism or anything on the autism spectrum, prepare immediately.

Here is how you prepare, you do all the research you can on whatever your child was diagnosed with and try to find other people you know who have experienced something similar either in their own life, or someone else's life. It's very important that you surround yourself with as much support and helpful tips and tricks you can get. It could make the whole difference between your child's success, or failure.

When I was diagnosed at age four my family immediately started to do as much research as possible on Asperger's. My grandmother bought a bunch of books, and my dad found these boys who to this day run this website called "Asperger Experts." The boys who run it both grew up with Asperger's. They gave my dad several helpful tips on how to help me. It was a true blessing. I highly recommend them if you have or know someone with Asperger's Syndrome. Some of the tips they provided were, make changes happen very slowly, and never underestimate the capabilities of your child.

That being said, when you begin to make any changes to your child's life, make it happen as slow as possible. This will make your child as comfortable and as flexible as possible going through the change. And remember, if they do get upset by it, it's okay to call them out, but NO strong discipline. Strong discipline is what will traumatize your kids. You must be just as flexible as you want them to be.

The next thing to remember is to never underestimate your child's capability. Parents of autistic kids tend to sometimes think their kids have limited capabilities. What I'd suggest is if there is a challenge that you don't know if your child can face, let them see the challenge, and if they don't go for it, ask them if they think they can do it or not. If they say no, then ask them if they think they could do it with help. If they then say yes, you obviously need to help them out. If they start to struggle even with help, you must be able to tell if they're actually trying or not. If they are trying it may be a good idea to put that challenge aside until later on. If they aren't trying, then you can gently push them to actually try and show them they can do it.

As your child gets to be about four or five, I'd try to find a young child autism center to get them plugged into. That would be a big help to them mentally because those people have experience with autism and know just how to treat it. Make sure it's specifically for your child's age group. And move them up accordingly.

When it's time for them to start school, do everything in your power to get them into either a special needs school, or homeschool them. I know that sounds like a stretch, but trust me, it's worth it. Make sure if you find a special needs school, that they aren't planning on making any gigantic changes like mine did. And if you plan on homeschooling your child. Make sure to find a curriculum that will best suit your child. Best ways to do that is the internet, I know, big shock.

If you for some reason can't get your child into a special needs school or you can't homeschool them, I highly recommend you talk with whatever school they are at and come up with a IEP plan and a way that they can work at their own speed. This may look like them spending the schooldays in a small classroom rather than a full one. And working alongside other special needs kids in that school.

This is what we attempted to do in my elementary school days. Now, I went to a very crappy elementary school. Not all elementary schools are like that. I just got very unlucky in that department.

Now even with all that put into motion you need to remember the socialization prospect of it all. Only let your kids socialize with people who won't bully them. That's why I recommended you hook them up with people who have similar disabilities. They will see that they can help and benefit each other. And it will be easy to make friends.

Now you may not be able to homeschool them yourself. There

however is a program where you attend virtual classes with REAL teachers. I don't remember exactly what grade it starts, but I do know that kids on the spectrum that go through it, have been known to be very successful. I know cause I'm one of them. It's called the WiloStar3D academy. It goes from whatever grade it begins at, to the twelfth grade. The best part about the whole thing, no bullies. All the students just cannot bully. If they did the messages they send can be seen by anyone in the administration. They will immediately expel the student and they will have lost the greatest opportunity they'd ever received for their high school education.

Okay, we've talked about what to do when your child is young. As they get older, here is what I recommend. Let's begin with support systems.

A growing child's support system is key to their growth with autism. I recommend you get them in to see a counselor. I didn't get into to see one for FAR to long. It was the worst thing we could've done, was wait as long as we did before getting me into a counselor. DO NOT WAIT. Get them in as soon as humanly possible. Even if it's simply a phone call every week. Get them a counselor NOW. Trust me, it won't just help their autism, it will help them mentally.

Now were going to talk about why counselors are a big help. They will teach us coping mechanisms.

Like breathing exercises or brain games. If you breath in for ten seconds, and out eight, after about twenty times of repeating that process you will have dropped your stress level a lot.

A good brain game that my counselor taught me was roleplaying. It could be with yourself, or with a family member. Regardless after you roleplay about a certain situation, you will have gotten stuff out of your head and processed them. That's very important to becoming more mentally stable.

Now I want to talk about not forgetting things. Unfortunately, loads of autistic people (myself included) have problems remembering things. The best way to combat this is to set reminders on your phone and handwriting stuff down on paper. This will increase your chances for remembering things by a long shot.

These are just a few examples of how you can help yourself, or anyone else you know who suffers from autism. It's very important to remember that were here for a reason. Autism is part of that reason for some people. We must remember to never frown upon those with disabilities. They are just as much a part of the future as we are.

Never forget God's word. He tells us that we are to take the gifts we've been given and use them for the greater good. Not to neglect them, or use them poorly. I hope you were able to take something away from this book. Rather it be a better understanding of autism, a closer connection to God, or even both. This book in a way really helped me. I was able to journal a lot of my past and that was a big release for me.

Journaling is a big part of getting relief from anything mentally. Writing down your thoughts does wonders. You just need to figure out how it will work for you. In my case, it was this book.

I really appreciate you taking the time to educate yourself on these matters. Share these thoughts around your community. Get them out in the open. The more you do that. The more people you will impact. It's very important to know when to take a stand. You never know when you could change someone's life.

Thanks for

reading.

God *Bless!!*

Notes

Notes

ACKNOLEDGEMENTS

Thank you to all those who have supported me during this process. Thanks to all those who took the time to read this book.

Thank you to Lulu for the outlet that it is for authors all over the world.

Thank you to my friends Luke, Marshall, Michael, Lily, the Wolf family, the Luck family, and my old classmates who know what it's like to go through life differently than most people.

Thank you to my parents and grandparents for all the support they've given me my whole life. I love you Nana and Papa, Mom and Dad.

ABOUT THE AUTHOR

Zachary Chapman is an aspiring writer from Orlando, Florida. He's a devout Christian, who loves rap music. He's been writing stories his whole life and hopes to get into a career in filmmaking. He is almost a senior in high school and is looking forward to his bright future. He currently works as an on the air personality on Hot 95.9 in O-Town. He lives with his dad, grandparents, dog, two cats, two gerbils, a leopard gecko, and a tank full of goldfish.